HOW TO DEAL WITH ONLINE TROLLS

Expert advice on handling cyberbullying

Steve Quinn

CONTENTS

CHAPTER 1 – TROLLS

Welcome to How to Deal with Online Trolls, a book that aims to help you navigate the world of social media and handle the inevitable trolls that come along with it. With the rise of online communication, it has become increasingly easy for individuals to hide behind screens and leave hurtful or negative comments towards others. This behaviour, known as trolling, can have detrimental effects on one's mental health and well-being.

In this book, we will explore what exactly constitutes as online trolling and why people engage in this activity. We will discuss the different types of trolls you may encounter on various social media platforms such as Twitter, Instagram, and Facebook. Additionally, we will provide you with practical tips and strategies for handling trolls including how to recognize when someone is trolling you, how to respond effectively without escalating the situation, and how to protect your mental health when dealing with negativity online.

Our goal is not only to help you deal with trolls but also empower you with the knowledge and skills necessary to create a positive online environment for yourself and others. By the end of this book, we hope you will feel equipped to handle any troll that comes your way while maintaining your sanity and dignity in the process.

In today's digital world, online trolling has become a major issue that affects individuals and society as a whole. Online trolls are people who post inflammatory or offensive comments on social media platforms, forums, and other websites with the intention of provoking others. The impact of online trolling can be significant, leading to mental health issues, harassment, and even suicide.

Definition of Online Trolls

The term "troll" comes from Norse mythology, where trolls were creatures known for causing mischief and mayhem. In the context of the internet, trolls are individuals who intentionally post inflammatory or off-topic messages in online discussion forums or social media with the aim of disrupting conversations and provoking emotional responses from others.

Trolling can take many different forms. It can involve insulting or mocking other users, spreading false information or rumours, creating fake accounts to harass others anonymously, or simply posting irrelevant comments that derail conversations.

Online trolls often hide behind anonymity to avoid consequences for their actions. They may create multiple accounts to amplify their message or make it appear as though there is more support for their views than there actually is. Trolls may also use bots to automate their attacks or flood comment sections with spam.

Types of Online Trolls

There are many different types of online trolls who use a range of tactics to provoke reactions from other users. Some common types include:

> The Insulter - Insulting other users' intelligence or appearance is one tactic used by online trolls to get a reaction out of people. These insults are often designed to be especially hurtful.

> The Flame Warrior - The flame warrior is someone who likes arguing for argument's sake. They don't necessarily

care about the topic at hand but enjoy getting into heated debates with anyone willing to engage with them.

➤ The Griefer - Griefers derive pleasure from ruining other people's enjoyment of an online community through disruptive behaviour, such as spamming or flooding chat rooms.

➤ The Doxxer - Doxxing involves revealing someone's private information online, often with malicious intent. This can include their name, address, phone number, or even their social security number.

➤ The Cyberstalker - Cyberstalkers engage in harassing behaviour that is designed to cause fear or distress to the person being targeted. They may send threatening messages or use doxxing tactics to expose personal information.

The Impact of Online Trolling on Individuals and Society

Online trolling can have a profound impact on individuals and society as a whole. For individuals who are targeted by trolls, the experience can be deeply traumatic. It can lead to depression, anxiety, and other mental health issues. In extreme cases, online harassment has been linked to suicide.

Trolls also have a negative impact on online communities more broadly. Their presence can prevent honest and open discussion from taking place, as people may be afraid of becoming targets themselves. This stifles creativity and innovation and prevents progress from being made on important issues.

In addition to the individual harm caused by trolls, there are also broader societal impacts to consider. Trolls often target marginalized groups of people based on factors such as race or gender identity. This reinforces existing power structures and perpetuates systemic discrimination.

Conclusion

Online trolling is a serious issue that affects individuals and society as a whole. With the anonymity provided by the internet, trolls can target people from all walks of life with little fear of consequences for their actions. It is important for platforms to take steps to address trolling behaviour and provide support for those who are targeted by it. By working together to combat this harmful behaviour, we can create safer online communities where everyone feels comfortable expressing themselves without fear of harassment or abuse.

CHAPTER 2 - THE PSYCHOLOGY OF ONLINE TROLLS

In this chapter, we will delve into the psychology behind online trolls. Understanding the motivations behind trolling behaviour and identifying the common personality traits of online trolls is crucial in dealing with them effectively.

Firstly, let's define what we mean by an online troll. An online troll is someone who intentionally posts offensive, inflammatory, or off-topic messages on social media platforms or forums to provoke a response or disrupt conversation.

To understand why people engage in trolling behaviour, we need to take a closer look at their motivations. According to research conducted by psychologists, there are several reasons why someone may become an online troll.

One of the main motives for trolling is anonymity. The internet provides a sense of anonymity that allows people to say things they wouldn't normally say in real life without fear of consequences. This can lead to individuals engaging in more provocative and aggressive behaviour than they would if their identity was known.

Another motive for trolling is boredom. Some individuals may engage in trolling behaviour because they have nothing else to do and find it entertaining.

Power and control can also be motivators for trolls. By provoking a reaction from others, trolls can feel like they have power over the conversation and control over the emotions of those involved.

In addition to understanding the motivations behind trolling behaviour, it's also important to identify common personality traits of online trolls. While not all trolls possess these traits, there are some characteristics that are often associated with trolling behaviour.

Narcissism is one trait commonly found in trolls. Narcissistic individuals have an inflated sense of self-importance and are often seeking attention and validation from others. Trolling can provide them with a platform to gain attention through negative means.

Machiavellianism is another trait found in many trolls. Individuals with this trait value manipulation and deception as tools for achieving their goals, regardless of how it affects others.

Lastly, psychopathy is a trait commonly associated with trolls. Psychopathic individuals lack empathy and are often impulsive and aggressive, which can lead to them engaging in trolling behaviour.

Identifying these common personality traits can be helpful in recognizing trolling behaviour and dealing with it effectively. It's also important to note that trolls may not always possess all of these traits, and some individuals may engage in trolling behaviour for different reasons.

In conclusion, understanding the psychology of online trolls is key to dealing with their behaviour effectively. By understanding their motivations and identifying common personality traits, we can recognize when someone is engaging in trolling behaviour and take appropriate action. Remember, it's important not to engage with trolls as it only fuels their behaviour. Instead, report their behaviour to the platform or forum moderators and focus on maintaining a positive online environment for yourself and others.

CHAPTER 3 – RECOGNIZING TROLL BEHAVIOUR

The internet can be a wonderful tool for information sharing and communication, but unfortunately, it also provides a platform for trolls to spread negativity and create havoc. Trolls are individuals who intentionally post inflammatory, off-topic or otherwise offensive messages online in order to provoke an emotional response from others. It's important to recognize troll behaviour if you want to effectively manage your online presence and navigate through the internet without getting sucked into their drama. In this chapter, we'll discuss how to distinguish between genuine disagreement and trolling behaviour, as well as some common tactics used by online trolls.

Distinguishing Between Genuine Disagreement and Trolling Behaviour

It's important to note that not all people who disagree with you online are trolls. In fact, healthy debate is encouraged in many online communities as it can lead to a better understanding of different perspectives. However, there are certain behaviours that distinguish genuine disagreement from trolling behaviour.

One common characteristic of trolling behaviour is the use of insults and name-calling instead of reasoned arguments. If someone is attacking your character instead of engaging with your ideas, they may be exhibiting troll-like behaviour. Another clue that someone is trolling is if they consistently take an extreme or unreasonable position on a topic just to cause conflict.

Pay attention to the tone of the conversation as well. If someone seems overly aggressive or confrontational right from the start of the discussion – particularly if you haven't interacted with them before – this could be another indication they're a troll. Additionally, trolls often derail conversations by introducing unrelated topics or repeating themselves excessively.

Common Tactics Used by Online Trolls

Now that we've covered some signs of trolling behaviour let's talk about some tactics that online trolls commonly use:

- ➢ Baiting - Trolls will often make provocative statements or ask loaded questions with the goal of triggering an emotional reaction from you or others in the group. This tactic is known as baiting. If you feel like someone is trying to goad you into an argument, it's best to ignore them.

- ➢ Gaslighting - Another tactic trolls use is gaslighting. This involves intentionally twisting your words or the meaning of a statement in order to make you look bad or crazy. If someone seems to be taking your words out of context or deliberately misinterpreting what you're saying, be cautious about engaging with them further.

- ➢ Doxxing - Unfortunately, some trolls will take their harassment offline by doxxing their victims. This involves publishing personal information about someone online with the intent of causing harm. If you're being targeted by a troll who has access to information about you, it's wise to take steps to protect yourself and your privacy.

- ➢ Fake accounts - Some trolls hide behind fake accounts in order to avoid consequences for their behaviour. They may create multiple accounts so they can continue harassing someone even if they get banned from one platform. Keep an eye out for suspicious behaviour such as profiles with no profile picture or active social media history.

➢ Hijacking conversations - Trolls often hijack conversations and turn them into arguments where their main goal is only to upset others. To prevent this from happening, consider setting clear boundaries at the beginning of a conversation (for instance, keeping the discussion on topic). You can also enlist moderators or administrators on platforms where this functionality exists.

In conclusion, recognizing troll behaviour is essential if you want to maintain a healthy and positive online presence. By distinguishing between genuine disagreement and trolling behaviour and learning about common trolling tactics used online – including baiting, gaslighting, doxxing, using fake accounts, and hijacking conversations – you'll be better equipped to handle any negative encounters that come your way on social media and other online platforms. Remember: don't feed the trolls!

CHAPTER 4 - RESPONDING TO ONLINE TROLLS

Dealing with online trolls can be an exhausting and frustrating experience. However, how you respond to them could make all the difference. In this chapter, we'll explore some strategies for responding to different types of trolls and recognize when it's best not to respond at all.

Strategies for Responding to Different Types of Trolls

1. The Insulter Troll

The insulter troll is one that will insult you and your content without providing any constructive criticism or feedback. They are just trying to get a rise out of you. The best approach with this kind of troll is simply to ignore them. It's likely they're looking for attention, so denying it may discourage them from bothering you again.

2. The Contrarian Troll

This type of troll is always contrary just for the sake of being difficult. They may come at you with opposing views or simply find fault in anything you say or do. One strategy for dealing with this type of troll is to try and find common ground on a few points before addressing their criticisms. Trying to understand where they are coming from and acknowledging their point of view can also help disarm them.

3. The Self-Appointed Expert Troll

The self-appointed expert troll is someone who believes they know everything about a particular topic and will try to prove that they are right, even if they're not. Oftentimes this type of troll has little credibility and likes telling others what they should do without listening themselves, which can be frustrating as it's hard to have a rational conversation with someone like that.

When dealing with these types of trolls, it's essential that you remain composed, don't feed into their arrogance by arguing back but rather challenge their responses and refrain from being drawn into arguments.

4. The Racist/Sexist/Homophobic Troll

These types of trolls use hate speech or derogatory language towards specific groups of people. It's important not to tolerate this kind of behaviour and report them to the social media platform immediately. Do not engage with these trolls as you will give them more power and publicity than they deserve.

Recognizing When it's Best Not to Respond at All

Sometimes, the best way to deal with trolls is not to respond at all. Here are a few situations where it might be better for you to stay mum:

1. The Troll is Complaining About Something You Can't Control

If a troll is complaining about something that is out of your control, like an issue with the social media platform itself or some other external factors, responding would be futile as there's nothing you can do about it. If they're just venting, let them do so without engaging with them.

2. The Troll is Just Seeking Attention

The troll may be seeking attention or validation for their opinions. So if you don't give them the attention they want, they'll eventually go away on their own without any escalation.

3. The Issue Isn't Worth Your Time

You need to assess whether a particular issue raised by a troll warrants your time and energy before deciding whether to respond or ignore it.

Conclusion

Dealing with online trolls can be challenging, but understanding how to respond effectively can help reduce stress levels and help maintain your reputation online.

Remember always to remain calm in your responses and don't stoop down to the level of the troll by using abusive language yourself.

It's also important to recognize when ignoring or blocking someone might be more effective than responding across different types of situations.

Don't forget that building a positive online profile takes time and effort, so keep that in mind when dealing with negative comments; keep focused on producing quality content rather than engaging in arguments with trolls who are only interested in wasting your time!

CHAPTER 5 - DEALING WITH CYBERBULLYING AND HARASSMENT FROM TROLLS

Social media is a virtual world that has given individuals the power to express themselves freely. However, this power can also be exploited by trolls who use it as a platform to harass and bully others. This chapter aims to provide valuable insights on dealing with cyberbullying and harassment from trolls.

Understanding the Legal Implications of Cyberbullying and Harassment

Cyberbullying refers to acts of bullying that take place through digital platforms, such as social media sites, text messages or emails. It encompasses different forms of online aggression, including sending threatening or abusive messages, posting embarrassing photos or videos, spreading rumours or lies about a person, creating fake accounts using someone else's identity, and more.

Harassment, on the other hand, involves persistent or unwanted behaviour that causes emotional distress or fear in the victim. This may include stalking someone online, invading their privacy by sharing their personal information publicly without consent or repeatedly contacting them despite being asked not to do so.

Both cyberbullying and harassment are serious offenses that can have severe consequences. In many countries, including the United States and the United Kingdom, these actions are punishable by law. If you ever find yourself being harassed or bullied online by a troll, it is crucial to understand your legal rights.

In some countries like the UK under the Protection from Harassment Act 1997 (PHA), perpetrators may face up to six months in prison for their first offense of harassment. If they are found guilty twice within ten years of their first offense, then they could face up to five years imprisonment. The PHA defines harassment as "a course of conduct which causes another person alarm or distress". The act doesn't limit harassment just on social media sites but includes phone calls texts emails letters and in person behaviour too.

Similarly, in the United States under Title IX law schools must take appropriate measures to remediate harassment and bullying, and failing to do so puts them at risk of legal action.

Steps to Take If You Are Being Harassed or Bullied by an Online Troll

If you are being cyberbullied or harassed online, it is essential to take immediate action. Here are some steps you can take:

➤ Document the harassment: Save any messages, emails, posts or comments that the troll has made towards you. This will provide evidence if you decide to pursue legal action against them.

➤ Block the troll: Most social media sites and messaging apps have a blocking feature that allows you to prevent someone from contacting you or seeing your profile.

➤   Report the behaviour: Social media platforms often have mechanisms in place for reporting inappropriate behaviour by other users. Make sure to report the troll's account and provide as much detail as possible about the incident(s).

➤   Seek support: Talk to someone you trust about what is happening, whether it's a friend, family member or a professional counsellor or therapist. They can offer emotional support during this challenging time.

➤   Consider taking legal action: If the harassment continues and causes significant distress or harm, consider seeking legal advice from an experienced lawyer who specializes in cyberbullying cases.

➤   Remember that self-care is critical - Practice self-care while going through this ordeal as it can be distressing and mentally exhausting dealing with trolls constantly. Self-care can help regulate emotions and maintain physical well-being.

In conclusion, cyberbullying and harassment from trolls are serious threats that can cause significant emotional distress and even put individuals' safety at risk. It is essential to understand your legal rights and take immediate steps when such incidents occur online. By documenting the behaviour, blocking the troll, reporting their account, seeking support from others, considering taking legal action if necessary and practicing self-care we hope this chapter has helped create greater awareness on how best deal with online trolls.

CHAPTER 6 - PROTECTING PRIVACY ONLINE

In this digital age, it's important to take extra precautions when it comes to your online privacy. Trolls can use personal information against you, whether it's for their own entertainment or as a way to harm you. In this chapter, we'll discuss strategies for protecting your personal information from trolls and the importance of securing social media accounts.

Protecting Personal Information

The first step in protecting your personal information is being aware of what you share online. Trolls can use any piece of information they find about you to harass, bully or stalk you. Therefore, be cautious when sharing anything that could identify you, such as your full name, phone number, email address, home address or school/workplace location.

When creating social media accounts, avoid using your real name as a username. Instead, use an alias or a nickname that doesn't reveal your identity. Moreover, don't post pictures or videos that show your face or any other identifiable features like tattoos or birthmarks. If possible, limit who can view your posts by adjusting the privacy settings on each platform.

Another essential step is avoiding oversharing on social media platforms. Don't reveal too much about yourself in public posts and comments such as where you live and work or upcoming events and travel plans. Remember that trolls can use any piece of information they find about you to track down where you are in real life.

Importance of Securing Social Media Accounts

Securing social media accounts is crucial when it comes to protecting yourself from trolls and other malicious actors online. A compromised account can result in stolen identity and sensitive data leakage which puts both personal safety and reputation at risk.

Start by choosing strong passwords for all of your social media accounts; avoid using the same password across multiple platforms since if one account gets hacked then others will also be compromised easily. Use long passwords with a mix of numbers, letters and symbols that are complex enough to resist brute-force attacks.

Multi-factor authentication (MFA) is another great tool for securing social media accounts. MFA adds an extra security layer to your account by requiring you to enter a code sent via email, SMS or mobile app in addition to entering your password. It makes it tougher for trolls and hackers to gain access to your account, even if they have your login credentials.

Don't forget to be vigilant about phishing scams. Phishing is the practice of tricking victims into giving away their login credentials or personal information by posing as a legitimate entity through email or text messages. Always double-check the sender's identity before clicking on any links or providing any sensitive information.

Lastly, keep all social media platforms updated with the latest security patches and software versions since these usually contain fixes for known vulnerabilities that attackers may exploit.

Conclusion

In conclusion, protecting your privacy online is essential when dealing with trolls and other malicious actors on social media platforms. Limit what you share online, use strong passwords and multi-factor authentication, be aware of phishing scams and keep all accounts up to date with the latest security patches. Always remember that prevention is better than cure and taking precautionary measures will help protect yourself from the harms caused by trolls online.

CHAPTER 7 - MANAGING EMOTIONAL RESPONSES TO TROLLING BEHAVIOUR

Dealing with online trolls is a stressful experience. It's easy to get carried away by negative emotions, such as anger, frustration, and disappointment when they start attacking you. But losing your cool can make things worse because trolls often thrive on your reactions. In this chapter, we'll discuss ways of managing emotional responses to trolling behaviour. We'll explore coping mechanisms for dealing with negative emotions caused by trolling behaviour and give tips on maintaining a positive mindset despite encountering negative situations.

1. Take a break

When someone attacks you online, it's tempting to respond defensively right away. But sometimes the best response is no response at all. A pause gives you time to collect your thoughts and cool off before deciding how best to respond. You don't want to say something in the heat of the moment that you will later regret.

If you find yourself struggling with negative emotions after reading a troll comment, try taking a break from social media or whatever platform that's causing distress for a while until you feel better. During this time, take care of yourself by doing something fun or relaxing like taking a walk outside, watching an uplifting movie or reading your favourite book.

2. Lean on friends and family for support

It's important to have trusted people in your life that you can rely on when dealing with stressful situations like online trolling incidents. Friends and family can serve as sounding boards allowing us to vent our frustrations without any judgment.

Suppose you're having trouble coping with negative emotions caused by trolling behaviour; reach out to close friends and family members whom you trust and respect for advice, support and reassurance.

3. Keep your mind busy with positive activities

One of the best ways to cope with negative emotions is to keep ourselves occupied with positive activities that help us stay busy and focused on other things besides the negativity online trolls bring.

For instance, instead of spending hours scrolling through social media, try spending time on other activities that bring you joy such as reading, exercising, or baking. By keeping your mind busy with positive activities, you are less likely to dwell on the negativity brought about by online trolls.

4. Practice self-care

Online trolling incidents can be emotionally taxing and may leave us feeling drained and exhausted. It's important to take care of ourselves physically and emotionally during these stressful times.

Some self-care tips include getting enough sleep, eating healthy foods as well as engaging in regular exercise. Remember also that it's okay to seek professional help if you require it.

5. Avoid Engaging With Trolls

Trolls' main aim is to get a reaction out of their victims; they want attention and will often say things just to provoke a response. The best way of frustrating them is not giving them what they want and ignoring their attacks altogether.

Instead of engaging with trolls online, focus on the people who support you and the positive aspects of your life outside social media platforms.

6. Focus on causes greater than yourself

Sometimes the negativity from online trolls can make it difficult for us to maintain a positive outlook on life. In such cases, focusing our energies on altruistic causes greater than ourselves can shift our mindset from negative to more positive ones.

For example, volunteering at an animal shelter or food bank can give us a sense of purpose and fulfilment which in turn helps keep us emotionally grounded when dealing with online trolling behaviour,

7. Have perspective

Finally, remember that online trolls' opinions do not define who we are as individuals or professionals - their comments are only reflections of themselves.

It's important to keep things in perspective when dealing with negative comments from trolls; treat each incident as an opportunity to improve your resilience without letting their words affect your self-worth or confidence.

In conclusion, managing emotional responses to trolling behaviour can be an ongoing struggle for many people who have experienced this negative aspect of social media. By adopting the above coping mechanisms, you can better manage your emotional responses to online trolling and maintain a positive mindset even in the face of negativity orchestrated by online trolls.

CHAPTER 8 - REPORTING TROLLS TO AUTHORITIES

Online trolls can make our online experience a living nightmare, especially when they start engaging in illegal activities or harassing us. In such cases, reporting them to authorities is the most effective way to protect ourselves and prevent them from harming others.

In this chapter, we'll explore the guidelines for reporting instances of harassment, cyberbullying, or illegal activities conducted by a troll. We'll also discuss the resources available for reporting such incidents and how you can use them effectively.

Guidelines for Reporting Instances of Harassment or Cyberbullying

Harassment and cyberbullying are serious issues that can harm individuals both mentally and emotionally. If you're being harassed online by a troll, it's your right to report it to the relevant authorities. Here are some guidelines on how to do so:

> ➢ Document the incident: Before taking any action against an online troll, it's important to document every incident of harassment or cyberbullying. Take screenshots of their comments or messages, record any abusive language used against you, and keep track of when these incidents occur.

➢ Report it to the platform: Most social media platforms have policies against harassment and cyberbullying. You can report any incidents of abuse directly to them by using their reporting tools. The platform will investigate your claim and take action if necessary.

➢ Contact law enforcement: If the online harassment involves threats of violence, doxxing (releasing private information about someone), stalking or other illegal activities you should contact local law enforcement immediately.

➢ Use third-party services: There are various third-party services that specialize in tracking down trolls and gathering evidence against them. You might want to consider using these services if you've had no luck with other options.

Resources Available for Reporting Incidents

There are several resources available for reporting online abuse and tracking down trolls:

➢ Social Media Platforms' Reporting Tools - Most social media platforms such as Facebook, Twitter, and Instagram have their reporting tools to report abuse or harassment. These tools are generally easy to use and allow you to report the incident anonymously.

➢ National Cybercrime Reporting Centre - This is a scheme in place in the UK that allows individuals to report cybercrime incidents quickly and easily. The centre works closely with local law enforcement agencies to investigate incidents of online abuse.

➢ Internet Crime Complaint Center (IC3) - IC3 is a partnership between the Federal Bureau of Investigation (FBI), the National White Collar Crime Center (NW3C), and the Bureau of Justice Assistance (BJA). It allows individuals to report internet-related crimes and provides them with resources on how to protect themselves from online trolls.

➢ Stop Online Abuse - This organization is a helpline for people who have experienced online abuse or harassment. They offer support, guidance, and practical advice on how to deal with trolls.

➢ Anonymous Reporting Services - There are several anonymous reporting services available that allow you to report cyberbullying or other forms of abuse without revealing your identity. For example, you can use Report Harmful Content to report any online material that promotes violence or hatred.

Conclusion

Dealing with online trolls can be challenging but it's important to take action against them especially when they start engaging in illegal activities or harassing us relentlessly. When dealing with trolls remember always document every incident of harassment, cyberbullying, or illegal activity conducted by the troll(s) as this will help authorities track them down more effectively.

Using social media platform reporting tools along with third-party services such as National Cybercrime Reporting Centre, Internet Crime Complaint Center (IC3), Stop Online Abuse, Anonymous Reporting Services can aid in getting justice for those affected by trolling online. Remember whenever possible keep evidence like screenshots of abusive comments & messages received as well recording any abusive language used against you so that these incidents can be shared with the relevant authorities.

CHAPTER 9 - STRENGTHENING MENTAL HEALTH WHILE DEALING WITH TROLLS

Dealing with online trolls can be a daunting and emotionally draining experience. The constant barrage of negative comments, hate speech, and cyberbullying can have a significant impact on your mental health. Therefore, it's essential to strengthen your mental health while dealing with trolls.

In this chapter, we'll discuss ways in which you can build up self-esteem and confidence in difficult situations. We'll also highlight the importance of practicing self-care techniques to help you maintain your well-being.

Building Up Self-Esteem and Confidence

When dealing with trolls, it's easy to feel like you're not good enough or that something is wrong with you. However, it's important to remember that their behaviour says more about them than it does about you. Here are some ways to build up self-esteem and confidence when dealing with trolls:

➤ Focus on Your Positive Attributes: It's easy to get caught up in the negative comments and forget about all the positive things in your life. Take some time to focus on your positive attributes and accomplishments. Write them down if necessary and read them every day as a reminder of how great you are.

➤ Surround Yourself With Positive People: Being around supportive friends and family can have a significant impact on your mental health. Reach out to those who lift you up when you're feeling down.

➤ Take Care of Yourself: Practicing good self-care habits such as getting enough sleep, eating healthy foods, exercising regularly, and taking breaks from social media can help boost your self-esteem and confidence.

➤ Set Realistic Goals: Setting realistic goals for yourself can provide a sense of accomplishment that can boost your confidence levels. Make sure these goals align with your personal values and beliefs.

➤ Practice Gratitude: Focusing on what you're thankful for can shift your mindset from negative to positive. Try writing down three things every day that you're grateful for.

Practicing Self-Care Techniques

Self-care is essential when dealing with trolls. It helps you maintain your well-being and cope with the stress and anxiety that can result from their behaviour. Here are some self-care techniques to consider:

➤ Take a Break: Taking time away from social media can help you recharge and refocus. Consider taking a break for a few hours or even a day, if necessary.

➤ Practice Mindfulness: Mindfulness practices such as meditation or deep breathing exercises can help reduce stress and anxiety levels.

➤ Seek Professional Help: If the trolling has become overwhelming, don't hesitate to seek professional help. A licensed therapist can provide additional support as you work through your emotions.

➤ Engage in Activities You Enjoy: Doing things you enjoy such as reading, listening to music, or spending time outdoors can provide a much-needed distraction from the negativity.

➤ Get Support From Others: Talk to friends and family about what you're going through. Having someone who listens without judgment can provide a sense of relief and validation.

Conclusion

Dealing with online trolls is never easy, but it's important to remember that their behaviour says more about them than it does about you. Building up self-esteem and confidence, along with practicing self-care techniques, can help you maintain your mental health while navigating through these challenging situations. Remember to take care of yourself first, and don't hesitate to seek professional help if needed.

CHAPTER 10 - BUILDING A SUPPORT NETWORK

Dealing with online trolls can be a lonely and isolating experience. It's easy to feel like you're the only one going through it, especially if your friends and family aren't familiar with the online world. But the truth is, there are many others out there who have also been targeted by trolls, and building a support network can be incredibly helpful.

Reaching out to others who have experienced trolling behaviour can provide a sense of validation and understanding. It's comforting to know that you're not alone, and that others have gone through similar experiences. Additionally, connecting with other victims of trolling can help you gain new insights into how to deal with it effectively.

So how do you go about finding others who have been trolled? One of the easiest ways is to search for online communities or forums dedicated to discussing trolling behaviour. These can include general social media platforms like Twitter or Reddit, as well as more specialized groups focused on specific topics or issues.

When searching for these communities, it's important to be strategic in your approach. Look for groups that are active and engaged, with members who are supportive and responsive to each other's experiences. You may also want to consider joining groups that align with any particular interests or hobbies you have - for example, if you're a gamer who has experienced trolling while playing online games, there may be specific gaming communities where you can connect with others who share your experiences.

Another option is to reach out directly to organizations or advocacy groups that focus on online harassment and abuse. These groups often provide resources such as counselling services, legal advice, and support networks specifically designed for victims of trolling behaviour.

One such organization is the Cyber Civil Rights Initiative (CCRI), a non-profit dedicated to fighting cyber harassment and stalking. In addition to providing support and resources for victims of online abuse, CCRI also advocates for stronger laws around cybercrime and works closely with law enforcement officials across the country.

Another organization to consider is the National Network to End Domestic Violence (NNEDV), which provides resources and support for victims of domestic abuse, including online harassment. NNEDV runs a project called Safety Net, which specifically focuses on helping survivors of domestic violence navigate technology safely and securely.

It's worth noting that while these organizations can be incredibly helpful, they may not be able to solve all of your problems. It's important to have realistic expectations about what they can offer, and also to remember that everyone's situation is unique.

Ultimately, building a support network is about finding people who understand what you're going through and can offer empathy and advice. Whether it's through online forums or advocacy groups, connecting with other victims of trolling behaviour can help you feel less alone and more empowered in dealing with this challenging issue.

CHAPTER 11 - AVOIDING TOXIC COMMUNITIES

As social media grows in popularity, so too does the prevalence of online trolls and toxic communities. These spaces can be incredibly damaging to your mental health and can take a toll on your overall well-being. Fortunately, there are ways to avoid these harmful environments and ensure safe digital interactions.

Identifying harmful environments

The first step in avoiding toxic communities is identifying them. These types of spaces often have a few common characteristics:

1. Lack of moderation

Communities that lack moderation or have lax moderation policies are more likely to attract trolls and allow for harmful behaviour. Look for forums or social media groups that have clear rules and active moderators who enforce those rules consistently.

2. Negativity

Toxic communities are often characterized by negativity, bullying, and harassment. If you come across a forum or group where members seem excessively negative or critical, it might be best to steer clear.

3. Closed-mindedness

Healthy communities encourage open discussion and debate, but toxic ones are often closed-minded, intolerant of differing opinions, and quick to attack anyone who thinks differently.

4. Conspiracy theories

Communities that embrace conspiracy theories or spread misinformation can be dangerous because they can lead to harmful actions or beliefs.

Strategies for ensuring safe digital interactions

Once you've identified potentially toxic online spaces, it's important to take steps to protect yourself from harm.

1. Limit exposure

One of the simplest things you can do is limit your exposure to these environments as much as possible. This might mean unfollowing certain accounts on social media or avoiding specific websites altogether.

2. Practice self-care

If you do find yourself in a toxic online space, it's important to practice self-care regularly. Take breaks from the platform if needed or engage in activities that help you feel calm and centred.

3. Engage thoughtfully

When engaging with others online, always aim to be thoughtful and empathetic. Avoid name-calling or attacking others, even if they are behaving poorly themselves.

4. Report harmful behaviour

If you witness harmful behaviour online, report it to the platform's moderators or administrators. Most social media platforms have specific reporting mechanisms in place for this purpose.

5. Seek support

Finally, don't be afraid to seek support from friends or mental health professionals if you're feeling overwhelmed by your digital interactions. Sometimes talking things out with a trusted confidante can help relieve stress and anxiety.

Conclusion

Avoiding toxic online communities is crucial for protecting your mental health and ensuring safe digital interactions. By identifying harmful spaces early on and taking steps to protect yourself, you can enjoy all the benefits of social media without the negative side effects that often come with it. Remember to prioritize self-care and empathy in all of your interactions online, and don't hesitate to seek help if needed.

CHAPTER 12
- MINDFUL
COMMUNICATION
PRACTICES

Trolling has become a widespread phenomenon on the internet. It is not uncommon to encounter people who are intentionally trying to provoke negative reactions or incite arguments online. As a result, online interactions can quickly spiral out of control, leading to misunderstandings and hurt feelings.

In this chapter, we will discuss mindful communication practices that can help minimize misunderstandings and improve the quality of online interactions. We will explore the importance of clear communication, active listening, and empathy in building positive relationships with others online.

Techniques for Minimizing Misunderstandings

Misunderstandings are one of the most common problems in online communication. They can arise from misinterpretation of tone or intent, lack of context or shared knowledge, or simply from differing perspectives. To avoid misunderstandings, it is important to use clear and concise language that conveys your meaning accurately and unambiguously.

One technique for minimizing misunderstandings in written

communication is to use simple language and short sentences that get straight to the point. Avoid using jargon or technical terms that may be unfamiliar to your audience. Try to anticipate potential areas of confusion and address them proactively by providing additional context or explaining key concepts.

Another technique for minimizing misunderstandings is to use visual aids such as images, charts, or diagrams that can help convey complex ideas more effectively than words alone. Visual aids can be especially useful when communicating with people who speak different languages or have limited reading comprehension skills.

Active Listening

Active listening is an essential skill for effective communication in any setting, but it is particularly important in online interactions where there are no visual cues such as body language or facial expressions to help convey meaning. Active listening involves paying close attention to what someone else is saying without interrupting or judging them.

One way to practice active listening online is to read carefully what someone else has written before responding. Take the time to understand their perspective and try to see things from their point of view. Avoid making assumptions or jumping to conclusions based on incomplete information.

Another way to practice active listening is to ask clarifying questions when you are unsure about someone else's meaning. This can help prevent misunderstandings and ensure that both parties have a clear understanding of the other's perspective. Examples of clarifying questions include: "Can you explain what you mean by that?" or "How does that relate to what we were talking about earlier?"

Empathy

Empathy is the ability to understand and share the feelings of another person. It is an important component of effective communication because it helps build trust and positive relationships with others. Empathy involves putting yourself in someone else's shoes and seeing things from their perspective.

One way to practice empathy in online interactions is to focus on the person behind the screen rather than the words on the screen. Try to imagine what they might be feeling or thinking based on their communication style, tone, and word choice. Avoid attacking them personally or making assumptions based on incomplete information.

Another way to practice empathy is to acknowledge and validate someone else's feelings even if you don't agree with their perspective. For example, you could say something like, "I can understand why you might feel that way" or "I appreciate your perspective even though I don't necessarily agree with it."

Conclusion

Mindful communication practices such as clear communication, active listening, and empathy are essential for building positive relationships with others online. By taking the time to communicate effectively, we can minimize misunderstandings and reduce the negative impact of trolling on our mental health and well-being.

Next time you find yourself engaged in an online interaction, take a moment to consider how you can apply these mindful communication practices to improve your communication skills and build more meaningful connections with others online. Remember that every interaction has the potential for positive change if approached mindfully and with respect for others' perspectives.

CHAPTER 13 - UNPLUGGING FROM SOCIAL MEDIA

Social media platforms have become an essential part of our daily lives. They keep us connected with the world, enabling us to share ideas, opinions and experiences with people from all around the globe. However, constant use of these platforms can be tiring and even harmful in some cases. One negative aspect of social media is the presence of online trolls who seek to cause trouble and harm others. In this chapter, we will discuss the benefits of taking a break from social media and strategies for making an effective break.

Benefits of taking a break from social media

Taking a break from social media can provide several benefits that can improve your mental health and wellbeing. Here are some of them:

➢ Reduce stress levels - Social media use can cause anxiety and stress in users by creating unrealistic expectations, negative comparisons, and constant notifications that are hard to ignore.

➢ Improve sleep quality - Late-night scrolling through social media feeds can disrupt sleep patterns, leading to insomnia or fatigue during the day.

➢   Increase productivity - Social media is one of the biggest distractions for workers today, contributing to procrastination and reduced productivity levels.

➢   Enhance real-life relationships - Spending less time on social media allows you to focus more on building meaningful relationships in real life with friends and family members.

➢   Promote mindfulness - Taking a break from social media provides an opportunity for introspection, reflection, and mindfulness which helps reduce stress levels.

Strategies on how to make an effective break from social media platforms

Whether it's a temporary or permanent decision, stepping away from social media requires planning and preparation. Here are some tips on how to make it effective:

➢   Set goals - Before you unplug from social media, set specific goals that you want to achieve during your break such as spending more time outdoors or reading books.

➢   Notify your contacts - Inform your contacts about your decision to take a break and let them know how they can reach you if necessary.

➢   Use apps to track your usage - Several apps like Moment, Offtime, and Freedom can help you monitor your social media use by providing usage statistics or blocking access to certain sites.

➢   Replace social media with other activities - Use the extra time that you have from not using social media platforms to engage in other productive or leisurely activities such as exercising, cooking or learning a new skill.

➢   Find alternatives for communication - If you need to stay connected with certain people, make sure that you have alternative means of communication such as email, phone or messaging apps.

➤ Schedule regular check-ins - Set specific times during your break to check in on your accounts for any important updates or messages so that you do not feel completely disconnected from the world.

➤ Reflect on your experience - After your break, reflect on what you learned about yourself and others while being unplugged from social media. This will help inform future decisions regarding social media use.

In conclusion, taking a break from social media is a healthy way of dealing with online trolls who may cause harm and negativity in our lives. It provides an opportunity for introspection and reflection which helps reduce stress levels, improve sleep quality and increase productivity levels. Making an effective break requires planning and preparation that includes setting specific goals, notifying contacts of your decision, finding alternatives for communication and scheduling regular check-ins among others. It is important to reflect on the experience after the break so that we can make informed decisions about our future use of social media platforms.

CHAPTER 14 - FIGHTING BACK WITH POSITIVITY

When it comes to dealing with online trolls, one of the most effective ways to combat their negativity is by promoting positive and constructive conversations. It may seem futile at times, but spreading positivity can have a ripple effect that inspires others to do the same. In this chapter, we will explore ways to fight back against online trolls with positivity and why using social media as a tool for good is crucial.

Firstly, let's discuss some ways to promote positive and constructive conversations online. One way to do this is by choosing your words carefully. When responding to negative comments or engaging in discussions, try to use language that is respectful and empathetic. Avoid using aggressive or inflammatory language as this can escalate tensions and lead to even more negativity.

Another way to promote positivity is by acknowledging when someone has made a valid point or raised an important issue, even if you disagree with them. By showing respect for other people's opinions and being open-minded, you can create an environment where people feel comfortable sharing their thoughts without fear of judgment or ridicule.

It's also important to remember that social media platforms are not just spaces for venting frustrations or arguing with strangers – they can also be used as powerful tools for creating positive change. By highlighting inspiring stories and initiatives, sharing resources that promote wellbeing and mental health, or simply posting thought-provoking content that encourages reflection and self-improvement, we can help shift the narrative towards more positive outcomes.

Now let's talk about the importance of using social media as a tool for good. With so much negativity on these platforms – from cyberbullying and hate speech to fake news and conspiracy theories – it's easy to become disillusioned with their potential for positive impact. However, when used responsibly and intentionally, social media can be a powerful force for good.

One example of this is the #MeToo movement, which began as a hashtag on Twitter in 2017 before spreading across various social media platforms. By encouraging people to share their stories of sexual harassment and assault, the movement sparked a global conversation about the pervasiveness of these issues and brought them to the forefront of public consciousness.

Similarly, social media has been instrumental in promoting various causes and initiatives, from environmental activism and LGBTQ+ rights to mental health advocacy and education reform. By providing a platform for people to connect with like-minded individuals from around the world, social media can help amplify voices that might otherwise go unheard.

Of course, using social media as a tool for good requires more than simply sharing uplifting content or getting involved in online activism. It also involves being mindful of our own behaviour on these platforms – how we interact with others, what we choose to share or promote, and how we use our influence to affect change.

One way we can do this is by being proactive about cultivating positive relationships online. This means engaging with others in a respectful manner, showing empathy towards those who may be struggling or experiencing hardship, and actively seeking out opportunities to support others through acts of kindness or generosity.

We can also use our social media platforms as vehicles for change by amplifying important messages and raising awareness about pressing issues. This might involve sharing articles or videos that shed light on injustices or inequalities around the world, posting petitions or calls-to-action that encourage people to take action against systemic problems, or simply using our own voice and influence to advocate for positive change.

In conclusion, while it may seem daunting at times to combat negativity on social media – particularly when it comes from trolls who seem intent on spreading discord – there are ways we can fight back with positivity. By promoting respectful and constructive conversations online, acknowledging other people's perspectives even when we disagree with them, and using social media as a tool for good rather than simply venting frustrations or arguing with strangers, we can create meaningful change in the world around us.

CHAPTER 15 - ONLINE ETIQUETTE FOR RESPECTFUL DISCOURSE

In an age where social media platforms are a ubiquitous part of our everyday lives, it's important to remember that the way we interact with each other online can have real-world consequences. Unfortunately, not everyone adheres to the same standards of online etiquette and respectful discourse. As such, it's important for all of us to take responsibility for maintaining a culture of civility on these platforms.

So, what are some guidelines for respectful interactions across different online platforms? Here are some key principles to keep in mind:

1. Be mindful of tone

The way you say something matters just as much as what you're saying. Avoid using aggressive or confrontational language when engaging with others online. Instead, approach conversations with an open mind and try to understand where the other person is coming from.

2. Stay on topic

When engaging in discussions online, try to stick to the topic at hand rather than getting side-tracked by other issues. This will help ensure that everyone stays focused, and that meaningful dialogue can take place.

3. Be respectful

Above all else, treat others with respect and kindness. Avoid personal attacks or insults, even if you strongly disagree with someone's point of view.

4. Acknowledge others' opinions

Even if you hold different views from someone else, it's important to acknowledge and respect their right to hold their own opinions.

5. Use evidence-based arguments

When making arguments or debating ideas online, try to use evidence-based approaches rather than relying solely on personal feelings or beliefs.

6. Don't feed the trolls

Online trolls thrive on conflict and negative attention – don't give them what they want! If someone is being abusive or disruptive, simply ignore them or report their behaviour to the appropriate authorities.

Of course, these guidelines aren't meant to be exhaustive – there are many other factors that contribute to respectful interactions online. However, by keeping these principles in mind, we can all work together towards creating a more harmonious online environment.

It's also important to remember that we all have a role to play in encouraging others to observe these standards of online etiquette.

Here are a few approaches you can take:

1. Model respectful behaviour

The old adage "actions speak louder than words" applies here – by modelling respectful behaviour yourself, you can set an example for others to follow.

2. Encourage positive interactions

When you see someone engaging in respectful discourse online, take the time to acknowledge and praise their behaviour. This will help reinforce the value of civility and encourage others to follow suit.

3. Call out bad behaviour

If you see someone engaging in abusive or disrespectful behaviour online, don't be afraid to call them out on it. However, do so in a calm and measured way – attacking them back won't solve anything.

4. Report problematic users

Most social media platforms have mechanisms in place for reporting abusive or disruptive users. If you encounter someone who is engaging in unacceptable behaviour, report them using these channels.

Ultimately, it's up to all of us to work towards creating a culture of respect and civility on our social media platforms. By following these guidelines and encouraging others to do the same, we can make the online world a safer and more pleasant place for everyone.

CHAPTER 16 - SUPPORTING OTHERS WHO HAVE BEEN TROLLED

In this chapter, we will focus on the importance of supporting others who have been trolled. Being targeted by trolls can be extremely distressing for an individual and it is important that they receive support from those around them.

Tips on offering emotional support:

➢ Listen attentively: The first and most important thing you can do for someone who has been trolled is to simply listen to them. Give them your undivided attention and let them express their feelings without interruption or judgement.

➢ Empathy: It is important to show empathy towards the person who has been targeted by trolls. Try to put yourself in their shoes and imagine how you would feel if you were in their position.

➢ Assure them: Let the person know that what happened was not their fault and that they are not alone in this situation. Trolling incidents can often make people feel embarrassed or ashamed, so it's crucial to assure them that there is no reason for shame or guilt.

➤ Encourage self-care: Encourage the person to take care of themselves physically and emotionally during this difficult time. Suggest taking a break from social media or engaging in activities they enjoy doing.

Techniques for encouraging others to seek help or report incidents:

➤ Raise awareness: Educate people about different types of trolling behaviours and why they're unacceptable both online and offline. Raising awareness about trolling behaviour can encourage more individuals to speak up against it when they witness it happening.

➤ 2.Support reporting mechanisms: Remind those who have been trolled about reporting mechanisms available through social media platforms or other relevant authorities such as anti-trolling organizations etc.

➤ 3.Promote professional help: Recommend seeking professional assistance if needed including counselling sessions with professionals familiar with mental health concerns arising due to internet-based harassment.

➤ 4.Encourage a positive perspective: Help your friend/ family member to think positively about their situation. Encourage them to view the situation in a proactive way and suggest that they turn the experience into an opportunity for advocacy or activism.

It is important to note that supporting someone who has been trolled can be emotionally taxing, particularly if you're close to them. You need to take care of yourself too while providing emotional support.

We hope these tips will help guide you when providing emotional support and offering assistance to those who have been trolled.

Remember, being supportive during this time is necessary as it can make all the difference in someone's life.

CHAPTER 17 - UNDERSTANDING THE ROLE OF BYSTANDERS

The internet is a breeding ground for all sorts of online behaviour, both good and bad. One such behaviour that has become increasingly rampant in recent years is trolling. Trolls are individuals who go around online forums, social media platforms, and blogs looking to harass, ridicule or simply annoy others with their comments. While trolls might only account for a small percentage of online users, their impact can be felt by many.

Dealing with trolls is never easy, especially when you find yourself caught up in the crosshairs of their attacks. However, what makes it even more difficult is when you have to contend with the silent bystanders who watch from the side-lines without doing anything to intervene. Such individuals might not be actively attacking anyone themselves but still contribute to the toxic environment that allows trolling to thrive.

Recognizing the impact of silent bystanders in toxic online environments

Silent bystanders play a crucial role in online environments where trolling is prevalent. They might not engage in trolling themselves but provide tacit approval for those who do by not speaking up against them. This can make it easier for trolls to continue engaging in their harmful behaviour because it creates a sense that no one sees anything wrong with it.

Moreover, by failing to intervene as a bystander witnessing trolling behaviour, you risk becoming part of the problem rather than part of the solution. The silence on your part could imply that you condone the negative behaviour and encourage its growth.

Tips on how to respond as a bystander witnessing trolling behaviour

As a responsible online user, it's essential always to speak out against any form of bad behaviour witnessed online, including trolling. Here are some tips on how to respond as a bystander:

➤ Don't ignore it - Ignoring bad behaviour and wishing it away will only make things worse. Instead, take an active stand against it and speak out against any harmful actions witnessed.

➤ Speak up - When you see trolling or other negative behaviour, speak up immediately to indicate that such actions are not acceptable. You can do this by leaving a comment on a forum or social media post, reporting the behaviour to site administrators, or privately messaging the offender.

➤ Choose your words carefully - It is easy to get caught up in the heat of the moment and respond with harsh language, but this may only escalate the situation. Instead, choose your words wisely and try to address the issue calmly and clearly.

➤ Offer support - If you witness someone being trolled online, consider offering them support. This could be through direct messages, comments or simply liking their posts. This small act of kindness can go a long way in making them feel less alone and more supported.

> ➢ Hold trolls accountable - Online trolls thrive on anonymity and often think they can get away with their misdeeds without consequences. However, if you hold them accountable for their actions by reporting their behaviour to site administrators or law enforcement officers where necessary, it sends a strong message that such behaviour will not be tolerated.

Conclusion

Silent bystanders play an instrumental role in either encouraging or discouraging negative online behaviours like trolling. As an online user committed to fostering positive online interactions, it's essential always to speak out against any harmful action witnessed. By doing so, we create a safer and more supportive environment where everyone can thrive without fear of harassment or ridicule.

CHAPTER 18 - THE FUTURE OF ONLINE COMMUNICATION

The world of online communication has come a long way since the early days of the internet. From chat rooms to social media platforms, technology has enabled people to connect with each other in new and exciting ways. However, with the rise of these new digital platforms, so too have we seen an increase in negative behaviour, such as trolling.

Trolls are individuals who intentionally post inflammatory or off-topic messages online with the goal of provoking other users into engaging in heated arguments or confrontations. Unfortunately, trolls can be difficult to deal with and can quickly turn a positive online space into a toxic environment.

Thankfully, technology is evolving in response to this issue. In recent years, many social media companies have implemented measures to address trolling behaviour and protect their users. For example, Facebook now allows users to report posts that they believe are offensive or abusive. Similarly, Twitter has introduced a feature that allows users to mute or block accounts that they do not want to interact with.

Beyond these specific features, there have also been broader technological advancements that could help address trolling behaviour. One such advancement is machine learning technology which is used by many social media companies to identify and remove harmful content automatically. By using algorithms trained on large datasets of past troll behaviour, this technology can detect patterns that might not be immediately apparent to human moderators.

Another promising development is blockchain technology which could potentially help prevent trolling by creating more secure and decentralized communication systems. With blockchain-based messaging apps like Dust Messenger and Obsidian combining encryption with peer-to-peer networking technology, it becomes much harder for trolls to disrupt conversations or infiltrate groups.

There are also several predictions for how the landscape of digital communication will continue to change in response to trolling behaviour. One likely trend is an increased emphasis on user privacy and security. As trolls become more sophisticated in their methods, users may become more cautious about sharing personal information online or engaging in public discussions.

In addition, we may see further development of tools and platforms that enable more focused and personalized communication. Rather than participating in large public forums where trolling behaviour can be prevalent, users may opt for more private or selective groups with stricter moderation policies.

Another potential development is the rise of gamification as a strategy for dealing with trolls. Online gaming platforms have long dealt with issues related to disruptive behaviour, and many have implemented features like ranking systems or rewards for positive engagement as a way to incentivize good behaviour. Social media companies could similarly introduce gamification elements in order to encourage users to post helpful, constructive content and discourage trolling.

Of course, predictions about the future of online communication are always subject to change. New technologies emerge constantly, and it is impossible to predict how they will be used or how they will impact different aspects of our lives. Nonetheless, it is clear that the issue of trolling behaviour is not going away anytime soon, and that new solutions will continue to be developed in response.

Overall, it is encouraging to see that technology is being leveraged in innovative ways to address the challenge of trolls online. While there is still much work to be done, these developments offer hope that we can create safer, more positive digital spaces for everyone. Whether through machine learning algorithms or blockchain networks, the future of online communication looks bright indeed.

CHAPTER 19 - ADVOCATING FOR CHANGE

As we've discussed throughout this book, dealing with online trolls can be a frustrating and often challenging experience. While there are certainly steps you can take to protect yourself and mitigate the damage caused by trolling behaviour, it's important to remember that these actions only address the symptoms of a much larger problem.

At its core, trolling is a form of harassment and abuse that has no place in digital spaces or anywhere else. To truly combat this behaviour and create a safer, more inclusive online environment for everyone, it's essential that we advocate for change on both an individual and systemic level.

One of the most important ways we can do this is by supporting policies and initiatives that aim to prevent and punish trolling behaviour. This could involve working with lawmakers to create stronger laws against online harassment or supporting organizations that provide education and resources to help people recognize and respond to trolling behaviour.

Another key component of advocating for change is promoting positive digital citizenship. This means encouraging individuals to take responsibility for their own actions online, treat others with respect and empathy, and actively work towards creating a more positive online community.

So what exactly does advocating for change look like in practice? Here are some actionable steps you can take:

Support anti-trolling policies: As mentioned earlier, one powerful way to combat trolling behaviour is by supporting policies that specifically address this issue. This could involve contacting your local representatives or signing petitions in support of anti-harassment laws or initiatives.

Join forces with community advocates: There are many organizations out there that are dedicated to promoting safer, more inclusive digital communities. By getting involved with these groups - whether through volunteering or simply attending events - you can help amplify their messages and make your voice heard.

Be an active bystander: If you witness someone engaging in trolling behaviour online, don't just sit back and let it happen. Speak up! Call out the person's behaviour as unacceptable and offer support to the person being targeted. By showing that trolling behaviour has consequences and that there are people who won't stand for it, you can help create a culture of intolerance towards this type of abuse.

Lead by example: Finally, perhaps the most powerful way to advocate for change is simply to be a positive force online yourself. Treat others with kindness and respect, engage in constructive conversations even when you disagree with someone, and always remember that behind every username is a real person with real feelings. By showing others what it means to be a good digital citizen, you can inspire them to do the same.

Of course, advocating for change can be challenging work. It requires persistence, dedication, and a willingness to confront uncomfortable truths about the state of our digital world. But it's also incredibly rewarding - not just because of the impact you can have on others, but also because of the positive changes you'll see in yourself as you work towards creating a better online community.

Remember: trolls thrive on negativity and chaos. If we want to truly defeat them and make our digital spaces safer for everyone, we need to focus on building up positivity, empathy, and respect - one action at a time.

CHAPTER 20 - CONCLUSION

Congratulations! You've made it to the end of this book on dealing with online trolls. By now, you should have a good understanding of what trolls are and how they operate, as well as strategies for coping with and neutralizing their negative behaviour.

To recap some of the main ideas that we've discussed throughout this book, here are some key strategies for dealing with online trolls:

➤ Don't feed the trolls: Trolls thrive on attention and will often escalate their behaviour if they sense that they're getting a reaction from you. It's important to resist the temptation to engage with them or respond to their comments, especially if they're being intentionally provocative or insulting.

➤ Report abusive behaviour: If a troll is being outright abusive or making threats, it's important to report them to the platform where the interaction is taking place. Most social media platforms have reporting tools in place for this purpose.

➤ Use humour and positivity: Sometimes a little bit of levity can go a long way in disarming trolls and diffusing negative situations. Using humour or positive language can help reframe the conversation and shift the focus away from negativity.

➢   Block or mute offenders: If an individual is repeatedly trolling you, it may be best to simply block or mute them so that you don't have to deal with their negative behaviour anymore.

➢   Seek support: Dealing with online harassment can be incredibly stressful and overwhelming, especially if it's happening on a regular basis. Don't hesitate to reach out to friends, family members, or mental health professionals for support during these difficult times.

Now that you have these strategies in mind, it's time to put them into action! Remember that dealing with trolls is not something you have to face alone - there are millions of people all over the world who are dealing with similar issues every day.

If there's one overarching message, we hope you take away from this book, it's this: you deserve to have positive and fulfilling digital experiences. While dealing with trolls can be challenging, it's important to remember that they are not representative of the vast majority of people online.

At the end of the day, it's up to each individual to determine how they want to engage with others in digital spaces. You have the power to create positive change by modelling respectful and empathetic behaviour, and by refusing to tolerate negativity or harassment from others.

As we come to the end of this book, I hope that you have learned a lot about handling online trolls. These individuals can be difficult to deal with, and they often thrive on creating chaos and negativity in our lives. However, by following the tips and strategies outlined in these pages, you will be better equipped to handle their attacks with grace and confidence.

Remember, when dealing with online trolls, it's important to stay calm and avoid engaging in their toxic behaviour. Instead, focus on building a positive online community by surrounding yourself with supportive friends and followers who share your values.

Ultimately, dealing with online trolls is all about staying true to yourself and not letting their words get the best of you. By practicing self-care techniques like meditation or journaling, you can strengthen your mental fortitude and remain resilient against their attacks.

So go forth with confidence and positivity, knowing that you've equipped yourself with practical strategies for dealing with online trolls. Here's to a brighter and more harmonious online world!

Thank you for reading this book! I hope that it has been a valuable resource for you as you navigate the sometimes-challenging world of social media. Together, we can create a safer and more welcoming space online for everyone to enjoy.

ABOUT THE AUTHOR

Steve Quinn

Steve is a prolific author of many books on marketing, branding, business management and social media etc. He brings over 25 years experience to the table, creating many online shops and businesses along the way. Despite his busy schedule, he finds time to enjoy the simple pleasures in life. He is an avid gardener, and enjoys spending time at home on his small farm.

www.ingramcontent.com/pod-product-compliance
Lightning Source LLC
LaVergne TN
LVHW051614050326
832903LV00033B/4491